VINTAGE SCARBOROUGH

Bryan Berryman

A companion volume to 'Scarborough As It Was'

Front cover: Scarborough Spa in the 1930's.
Alick Maclean conducts the Orchestra.

First edition – June 1976
Second impression – April 1983

Published by Hendon Publishing Co., Ltd., Hendon Mill, Nelson, Lancs.

© **Bryan Berryman 1976**

**Printed by Fretwell & Brian Ltd., Healey Works, Goulbourne Street,
Keighley, West Yorkshire BD21 1PZ.**

The author:
Bryan Berryman, B.A. (Durham), A.L.A.
has been reference and Local History
Librarian at Scarborough Public Library
since 1969. His other works include . . .
the County Durham Volume in the
King's England series, published in 1969
by Hodder & Stoughton, and numerous
articles on local history in the Durham
County Advertiser and the Scarborough
Mercury.

Acknowledgement:
Without the ready co-operation
of Mr. Peter W. Dove, who has
supplied many of the photographs, this book would not
have been published. the
Author owes him a debt of
gratitude.

Introduction

"By 1900 Scarborough had become a spectacle, the continuous Diamond Jubilee celebration of a spectacular Empire on holiday."

V. S. Pritchett

"It is odd, and sad, to find this native town of mine air-raid-sheltered, and patrolled by crash-helmeted A.R.P. men; to find the Spa closed and labelled 'Private' at this time of year; to realise the disappointment of landladies, whose houses are crowded with evacuees from Hull and Grimsby."

B. C. Hilliam ('Flotsam')

A beginning . . . and an end. Between these two reminiscences lie forty years in the history of one of Britain's leading seaside resorts.

This collection of photographs is an attempt to recapture something of the spirit and atmosphere of Scarborough between the Boer War and World War II. In those years, if we are to believe the newspapers and guidebooks of the day, Scarborough had few rivals for summer gaiety, fashion, style and good taste; and so in these pictures we see not merely the changing face of a northern provincial town, but a nation enjoying its leisure, often against a sombre background of unemployment, depression, and social inequality.

Generations of holidaymakers have pleasant memories of this Yorkshire resort; they will not deny the simple truth well-known to the Victorian excursionist, and sung on the beaches with cheerful energy by troupes of nigger minstrels and white-faced pierrots:

*"There is no place like Scarborough,
Scarborough By The Sea."*

From the Guidebooks

"Scarborough presents a combination of attractive features not excelled by any of the rival health resorts. Bracing air, an equable temperature, mineral springs of high medicinal value, splendid sands, romantic cliffs, excellent bathing, boating and fishing, a good system of drainage, great freedom from zymotic diseases, a low death-rate and an excellent train service.

. . . It is worth walking to the top of Oliver's Mount with unboiled peas in your shoes to obtain the exquisite sensations obtainable in feasting the eyes and storing the mind with the glories of so wondrously rich and unforgettable a panorama." 1899.

"Scarborough was an aristocratic resort much more than a century ago, and it is a fashionable town today. Refinement and good taste is the rule throughout, though it is a mistake to think that every male visitor must needs wear a frock coat and silk hat." 1902.

"'Life' in Scarborough is of a very sophisticated, not to say treadmill character. Everyone feeds at the same hours; everybody goes to the Spa at the proper times; most do a little fishing and a little flirting, and wind up with a concert and dance." 1907.

"Visitors whose means are limited will find good, clean and comfortable lodgings at prices ranging from 2½ to 5 Guineas a week in North Marine Road, Brunswick Terrace, Aberdeen Walk, Albemarle Crescent, Alma Square and Trafalgar Square. Perfectly respectable lodgings at yet cheaper rates may be had in Victoria Road and the streets leading therefrom. Bedroom and sitting-room accommodation may here be obtained at as low a figure as £1 or £1 10s. a week, but of course for such prices little in the way of attendance or elaborate furnishings must be expected," c.1900.

Some Vintage Headlines...

Scarborough Evening News 11 July 1925: SCARBOROUGH'S GREATEST ENEMY. Is it the Scarborian? Visitors still being locked out at night . . . . News of the World 6 August 1925: LURE OF SCARBOROUGH. TOWN OF A THOUSAND ATTRACTIONS. Where they bathe to musical accompaniment . . . . Leeds Mercury 21 June 1927: 1827 AND 1927 SHAKE HANDS. Joyous Scarborough Pageant. History relived in top gear . . . . Daily Chronicle 10 August 1927: "CONTINENTAL SCARBOROUGH." Leafy Haven of the Yorkshire Coast. Most civilised of all seaside resorts . . . . Yorkshire Weekly Post Illustrated 1 August 1931: SCARBOROUGH WOMEN ARE CAREFREE. Meet The One with Orange Pyjamas. No Grundyism . . . . Daily Mail 20 May 1932: BEETHOVEN BY THE SEA. Spa Orchestra Magic. Where "highbrow" music pays . . . . Northern Echo 23 June 1932: SCARBOROUGH'S ROSE QUEEN CROWNED. Gay Scenes Of Pageantry In Brilliant Sunshine. A retinue of pink . . . . Yorkshire Evening Post 26 April 1933: PLUS FOURS ON THE SPA. Scarborough Mayor Does Not Approve . . . . News Chronicle 24 July 1939: SCARBOROUGH OFFERS THE "BEST OF BOTH WORLDS." Sedate 1900's or Gay 1939's.

Vintage Fare

Information and tariff appearing under heading:

Scarborough South Sands

GRAND REFRESHMENT ROOMS

Specially adapted for Excursionists

Men's Lavatories, 1d; Women's Cloak Room, 1d;

Parcels Office, 1d. per parcel

Bread and Cheese	3d.	Porter per glass	1½d.
Plate of Cold Meat	6d.	Superior Ale per glass	1½d.
Potatoes	1d.	Alsopp's Bitter Ale per glass	2d.
Bread	1d.	Soda Water	3d.
Pickles	1d.	Lemonade	3d.
Roll and Butter	2d.	Seltzer & Potash	4d.
Biscuit	1d.	Ginger Beer	2d.
Bun or pastry	1d.	Port or Sherry	4d.
Tea per cup	3d.	Gin, Rum or Brandy	3d.
Coffee per cup	3d.	Irish & Scotch Whiskies	
Roll	1d.	per glass	3d.
Butter	1d.	Cordials & British Wines	
Sandwich	3d.	per glass	3d.
Sausage Roll	3d.	Claret Vintage 1874	6d.
Butterscotch &c. per pkt.	6d.	Bitter Ale & Stout, per ½ bot.	4d.
		Cigars	from 1d.

Persons bringing their own Provisions will be provided with Plates, Knives, Forks, Mustard and Salt at a charge of 1d. each Person.

*   *   *

For Osbert Sitwell the balcony of the Pavilion Hotel (on the left of the picture) was "inextricably mingled with all my early impressions of pageantry." In 1902 at the age of nine he watched "the Boer War veterans, just returned after victory long delayed, arriving outside the station, and forming up with their bands preparatory to a march round the town."

Left: "Mammoth bathing vans, each one branded with the pill-maker's name . . . . cumbrous, prehistoric monsters, under doom of extinction, basking in the sunshine by herds on the shore, or drowsing patiently, hippopotamus-wise in the water."

E.C. Booth.

'The more we are together . . . .' On a bank holiday in the 1890's, 'a grey and un-numbered multitude' of excursionists throngs the South Bay.

Far left: Vintage Scarborough is here personified in the imposing figure of Alick Maclean. 1912 was the first of his 24 successive summer seasons as director of the Spa Orchestra. His daily concerts on the open air bandstand and in the Grand Hall gained for Scarborough an unchallenged reputation for the best in seaside music.

Left: On Sir Edwin Cooper's bandstand of 1813, Alick Maclean conducts a morning concert towards the end of his life. He died at the age of 63 in 1936, the year in which he was to have celebrated his silver jubilee at the Spa and also to have received a knighthood.

"An interesting but somewhat unsavoury sight is to be witnessed after a large catch of herring by walking round the harbours, where on every available space on the piers and jetties are grouped bare-armed Scottish fisher lasses, standing over barrels and boxes, and 'gipping' (i.e. removing the insides of the fish) with a dexterity little short of marvellous."

1920 guide.

Right: All the atmosphere of the herring season is captured in this picture of the harbour in 1927. Most of the drifters in view are from Lowestoft, the next port of call as the fleet followed the shoals of fish.

Top left: Scarborough's 'High Street' midway between the two world wars. This is Westborough looking west towards the railway station. To the left is Vernon Road; to the right, Aberdeen Walk.

Bottom left: The same air of quiet respectability pervades this view of Westborough, looking east towards Huntriss Row and Newborough in the mid nineteen-twenties.

Above: Reconstruction of the eighty-year-old Valley Bridge began in 1925, soon after this picture was taken. It was Scarborough's first major motor age development.

When the new bridge was officially opened on 26 July 1928, the civic party was preceded by local schoolchildren dancing the traditional Cornish Furry Dance. The Minister of Transport and his wife followed on foot, but more sedately.

Right: The Northway through road scheme followed the opening of the Valley Bridge. By October 1929 Westfield Terrace had been reduced to rubble. The Waverley Hotel soon followed, but not until 23 March 1936 was the Odeon Cinema opened on the site. Scarborough-born Charles Laughton performed the opening ceremony.

From the clock tower of the railway station on a summer Saturday in 1931, the camera captures a moment in transport history. Scarborough's trams ceased to run on 30 September of that year, driven out of existence by the motor bus.

Right: Gone are the pierrots, the bathing machines, the street trams; this is Scarborough in the mid-thirties, the heyday of the ballroom, the roller skating rink, and the sophisticated concert party.

Left: For five shillings the more intrepid visitor could see Scarborough from a two-seater saloon air taxi; flights were made from the old racecourse on Seamer Moor.

Above: From 1911 to 1932 this famous concert party, which started as the first mixed pierrot troupe – Royle's Imps – on the North Sands, held the stage each summer at the Floral Hall. At the Spa, from 1929 to 1939, Murray Ashford's Bouquets offered equally choice entertainment – "A bunch of refined personalities tied up with a ribbon of originality."

Left: Two pennyworth of fun and fascination at the old Sea Water Baths in Coronation year, 1937.

Right: The paddle steamer BILSDALE returns from a cruise to Filey Bay. This coal-fired vessel, built in 1900, sailed out of Scarborough each summer from 1925 to 1934.

Left: The new diesel-engined Royal Lady, capable of carrying 460 passengers, made the veteran BILSDALE look positively outdated. She made her first sea trips from Scarborough on 6 July 1934.

SCALBY MILLS NEAR SCARBOROUGH. 4265. C.W.W.

Right: "All the donkeys on the north side of Scarborough were cousins of Pegasus. I seem always to have ridden at full gallop over those sands to an inn (Scalby Mills) beside a beck that had wound its way safely from the moorland to the sea. Hence, after being refreshed with ginger beer at a penny a bottle and hokey-pokey at a penny a lump, we galloped back to the marina on the north side."

Compton Mackenzie.

Left: The families return to the simple pleasures of the North Sands after World War I. The promenade had been opened in 1912 at the same time as Peasholm Park.

Right: The invasion of Scarborough by the family car is well illustrated by this view of Peasholm Gap in the early thirties. Corner Cafe dates from 1925, the cliff lift from 1929.

Punch and Judy act out their traditional tale for a gang of young castle builders on the North Sands.

The first performace of 'Merrie England' on 28 July 1932, Edward German's opera was repeated in 1936, and again in 1945, to mark the return of peace. Other pre-war productions were Tom Jones in 1933, Hiawatha 1934, Carmen 1935, Faust 1937, Tannhauser 1938, and in 1939 The Bohemian Girl.

Sunday 13 May 1945. The Victory Parade and Thanksgiving Service at the railway station mark the end of World War II and the start of a new era.